Accounting

Step by Step Guide to Accounting Principles & Basic Accounting for Small business

Mark Smith

Additionally, the information in the following pages is intended only for informational purposes and should thus be thought of as universal.

As befitting its nature, it is presented without assurance regarding its prolonged validity or interim quality. Trademarks that are mentioned are done without written consent and can in no way be considered an endorsement from the trademark holder.

Table of Contents

14. NOV 23.

SSAL

Please return/renew this item by the last date shown
on this label, or on your self-service receipt.

To renew this item, visit **www.librarieswest.org.uk**
or contact your library

Your borrower number and PIN are required.

LibrariesWest

Introduction

Congratulations on downloading *Accounting* and thank you for doing so.

The following chapters will discuss everything that you need to know to get started with Accounting. We will start this guidebook out with an introduction about how accounting and bookkeeping are different, along with some of the most common terms you will use, to make sure we understand how this area works.

After that, we will take a look at the different parts that come with accounting. We will look at the different types of bookkeeping, how to create some of the financial statements such as the income statement and other documents required by the SEC and the different types of accountants, the importance of tax accounting, and some tips to help you get started.

Accounting is such an important part of a business. It ensures that your financial records are accurate and that you can comply with all the SEC and tax laws. Make sure to check out this guidebook to help you get started.

There are plenty of books on this subject on the market, thanks again for choosing this one! Every effort was made to ensure it is full of as much useful information as possible, please enjoy!

Chapter 1:

How Bookkeeping and Accounting Are Different

Before we get too much into this guidebook, it is important to note that accounting and bookkeeping is not the same thing. Bookkeeping is going to concentrate on simply recording all the financial activities of a business. Keeping track of these transactions, no matter what they are depending on that particular business.

The accountant can then take this information and help the company by analyzing, summarizing, and reporting the results of what they found. The product or accounting is information, and this information is vital to the management of a company for their operating as well as investment decisions. If the management doesn't know how much money the business has, how much inventory that business holds, and how many employees they have along with employee pay.

Every business, as well as a nonprofit entity, will need a reliable system of bookkeeping that relies on established principles from accounting. Accounting will often cover more topics compared to what you see with bookkeeping. Bookkeeping is just going to be the part where you keep records of your business, or where you record all of the information about financial activities and all transactions for that particular business.

What Is Bookkeeping?

Bookkeeping is a subset of the arena of accounting. The process of bookkeeping is when you gather, organize, and store all your financial information so the company has that information ready when needed. This can help a company to keep them organized and to help them know where their financial situation is at the time. Bookkeeping is so important because of two reasons. These reasons include:

- Being able to facilitate the day-to-day operations of the business.
- Helping to prepare tax returns, internal report for the managers of the company, and to prepare any financial statements that are needed.

Bookkeeping will often be known as recordkeeping too, and this is a good way to ensure that you are going to remember what this process is all about. Bookkeeping is the infrastructure of the financial information for a business. This financial information needs to always be complete, accurate, and as timely as possible. This is why many businesses choose to keep their bookkeeping up to date each month at the latest and then will complete financial documents every quarter and every year.

Bookkeeping is the complete method that helps a business keep track of all its transactions. It is the activity of making sure that every single financial transaction of that company is fully documented and will form a base for the work that the accountant will do. The purpose of working on your books for a business is to disclose the best picture of your expenditures or income when that period of accounting is over.

A business will hire a bookkeeper who is responsible for tracking and recording all the transactions that occur for that business. They would need to track information like the cash that comes into or out of the business, goods that are sold or purchased on credit, any expenses that the business incurs, and more. This all needs to be done in a timely manner.

The bookkeeping is going to capture all the transactions that occur during the day and write them out for the business to keep track of. They will look at things like purchases, sales, any returns on purchases, sales return, cash book, the journal and more. Then this information will be posted to the proper ledger after the trial balance is prepared.

For the most part, there are going to be two methods that you can choose for bookkeeping. These include:

- The single entry system
- The double entry system

Most businesses will choose to work with the double entry system. This method may take a bit longer, but it is a good way to check your work as you go. If the two sides don't come out to 0, then you know that something was put into the system wrong, and you can go fix it.

What Is Accounting?

When we look at the term accounting, we are looking at a term that is much broader compared to bookkeeping. This goes into developing the system that will control how the bookkeeping will go for the business. It will establish the controls to keep the system in place. Accounting can also analyze and recheck the information that was recorded during bookkeeping. To keep it simple, the accountant is going to give the orders and then the bookkeeping will follow them.

Accounting is going to encompass the problems in measuring how the finances of a business will go based on the current and predicted future economic activity. In addition, accounting is going to include the function of financial reporting of values and performance measures to the ones who need this information the most. For example, investors, managers of a business, and even others will depend on these financial reports to learn more about the condition and performance of an entity.

An accountant is going to be responsible for designing all the internal controls of the bookkeeping system you decide to use. This is important because it will minimize any of the errors that may happen when recording all the transactions that the business does. The larger the business, the more likely they will have these errors because of the sheer number of transactions they do. The accountant will put in some internal controls that will help to detect and determine any theft, fraud, embezzlement, or other types of behavior that is considered dishonest in record keeping.

Accountants can also take that information and prepare reports based on it. They may write out a variety of reports from the bookkeeping process including tax returns, financial statements, and other reports that are confidential and are only meant for the managers. Accountants even can measure out profits for a company, a task that is going to depend on how accurate the information is that the bookkeeping did before. With this information, as long as it is accurate, the accountant is able to measure sales revenue and expenses in order to determine how much was made or how much was lost to the business over a specific time period.

Accounting is simply going to be a business language will help to provide information about where a company is—financially. It is a complete procedure that is going to start with the recording of transactions, which the bookkeeping is able to do, and then ends when the accountant reports and creates these financial statements for any business.

In the world of accounting, the monetary transactions are going to be found and then recorded, and then the accountant will go through and group similar transactions together. This is done to help present the information to the users through the financial statement. After looking through the financial statements, the accountant can then share the results of these statements with anyone who is interested in them.

The purpose of using accounting is to make sure that there is an accurate view, on that is fair, for all these financial statements, no matter which user looks at them. These users could include the government, managers of the business, suppliers, creditors, employees, and investors. These statements can be organized in a manner that makes them easy to understand by these individuals and really explains the finances of the business for a particular year.

There are also different branches that come with accounting, and these will include:

Social responsibility accounting
Human resource accounting
Management accounting
Cost accounting
Financial accounting

The Main Differences Between Accounting and Bookkeeping

While we did discuss this a little bit above, there are some differences that you should be aware of between the field of bookkeeping and the field of accounting. Some of these differences include:

- Bookkeeping is the process of a business keeping proper records of all transactions that occur in an entity. Accounting takes this further by recording, measuring, grouping, summarizing, analyzing, and reporting the transactions for that company, making sure that they do so in monetary terms.
- The tasks that come with bookkeeping is going to be done with the help of the bookkeeping. The tasks that are done in accounting are done by the accountant.
- Financial statements are something that is important to accounting, but you won't find in bookkeeping.

- Accounting records are important because they are the basis for making some major decisions by the managers of a business. Most of the time bookkeeping records are not going to be enough to help make some of these big decisions.
- Bookkeeping just records the information so that it is available when needed. With accounting, this information is presented through a third party to provide a true and fair view of how the business is doing, how profitable they are, and what their current financial status is.

A Comparison Chart Between Bookkeeping and Accounting

What We Are Comparing	What It Is in Bookkeeping	What It Is in Accounting
Meaning	This is the activity of keeping track of all the financial transactions that a business goes through during the year.	This is an orderly recording as well as reporting any financial transactions or information of that business for a specific time period
What is it?	This is more of a section that is used in accounting	This part is the main thing and will help you to keep good track of all your records and can use that for smart decisions about the company.

Preparation of financial statements	This is not something that is done with the process of bookkeeping	This is part of the process in accounting.
Tools	Bookkeepers will usually rely on ledgers and journals to help them get their work done.	Accounting will rely on a few tools to help including the important financial reports that are needed to comply with the SEC rules
Methods and subfields	These are going to include the option of the business to work with either double entry or the single entry bookkeeping system.	There are many options here that would include cost accounting, management accounting, and other financial help for the business.
How it helps determine the financial position	Bookkeeping is not there to show what financial position the company is in at that time.	The job of accounting is to show, as clearly as possible, the financial position of that company.

Chapter 2:

Some Terms You Should Know

There are a few terms that you should learn before you get started with accounting. Learning these terms can make it easier to know what we are talking about in this guidebook and will ensure that everyone is on the same page. Some of the terms you should know for accounting include:

- Asset: An asset is something that the organization owns that can help it finish its mission. For a retail store, this could be something like the inventory in the back room. For a fast food restaurant, the stove or the grill could be an asset.

- Liability: The liability is going to be anything that the organization owes to someone else. If you owe wages to employees, it can be a liability. Taxes that you owe at the end of the year can be liabilities. Bills for inventory or any loans that you owe money on can be liabilities.

- Equity: The equity is going to be the measure of the claim of someone on the assets of the organization. This could be some of the liabilities and the investment by any owners of the business.

- Income: This is the money that comes into the organization from its operations in whatever line of business it does.

- Expense: This is the amount that the business will need to spend in order to properly carry out its operations. This will represent payments to asset and service providers.

- Distributions: This is any outflow of money over to the stockholders or the owners. It can also be bonuses to the employees.

- Cash flow: This term is going to represent the money that flows through the operation or the income minus the expenses. The amount that is left at the end of the time period is the profit.

- Overheard: The overhead is going to be the group of costs that are not directly associated with the major functions of the company but are still necessary to make the company reach its goals. This could include the rent of the company, hiring janitors, and more.

- GAAP: This stands for Generally Accepted Accounting Principles. This is the rules that accounting professionals need to follow to make sure they are providing an accurate description of all the financial activities of a company. The rules that come with GAAP will apply to all companies, no matter what they sell or what sector they are in.

- Accounting: Accounting is a broad term to cover analyzing and verifying any information that is recorded, establishing some controls to ensure a system is working the proper way and can help with making decisions based on the information that is found in bookkeeping. It is going to cover a lot more topics compared to bookkeeping.

- Bookkeeping: Bookkeeping is basically the process of keeping all the records of the business. It will include writing down any information about transactions, profits, cash flow, and even debts and other expenses. The bookkeeping will often just follow the orders that the accountant gives to them.

Chapter 3:

The Different Types of Accountants

Accounting professionals are able to find their employment in many different types of work settings. The type of work that the accountant can do is going to depend on the type of certification they have and how long they went to school among other things. Some of the different types of accountants that are common include:

CPA or Certified Public Accountant

A CPA is an upper-level accountant who is usually known as the recognized experts for accounting records, taxes, and financial standing of a company. While they do spend some of their time helping a business get prepared for their taxes, the CPA is often going to work much more in-depth with the finances of a company than just the taxes.

The CPA is often seen as a trusted advisor for the company, working to help all their clients make plans that reach financial goals, while also assisting in any other fiscal matters as needed this could include work like reviews, audits, forensic accounting, litigation services and consulting.

To become a CPA, an accountant needs to get a bachelor's degree from an accredited accounting program. Then they need to pass the CPA examination to obtain their certification.

Forensic Accountant

The next type of accountant that you may choose to become is a forensic accountant. These are the detectives when it comes to accountants. These professionals are going to take a look at the financial records and analyze them, to make sure that they follow all the standards and the laws for that field. Often a company is going to bring in this kind of accountant because they need someone who can uncover errors, omissions, or even fraud inside of the company.

This kind of accountant will need to possess many different skills. They need to be a numbers person and also have the curiosity of an investigator. They can often work during an investigation or as litigation support. Depending on the situation, it is possible for these accountants to end up at court proceedings as an expert witness.

To get this kind of job, you must have a bachelor's degree in accounting. And then it is a good idea to have some kind of certification as well. Most forensic accountants are going to earn their CPA credentials. And then some forensic accountants are going to become a certified fraud examiner or a CFE.

Auditor

Auditors are going to be the ones in charge of the accuracy of financial records in the company. Many organizations, whether they are a commercial business or a non-profit, will need to conduct an audit each year in order to make sure that their records are precise. Auditors are going to usually come into the business from outside of the company. This helps to make sure that the numbers are looked over without any bias at all. If the auditor worked directly for the company, they may, whether or not they meant to, miss out on something important in the books.

These professionals are going to do a lot of inspecting and investigating. They will look through financial statements, inspect the account books, organize and then maintain fiscal records, and then assess all the financial operations of the company. They can then provide some recommendations to help the business improve.

To get a job as an auditor, you must get a bachelor's degree in accounting. You may find that getting some kind of accounting certification can help you in this field as well.

Management Accountant

You can also choose to be a management accountant. When a business leader is trying to make some decisions that are important, they need to know how the company is doing financially. These leaders also need to check how their decisions could affect the financial health of the business. The management accountant can provide the business leaders with this information to ensure that they make the sound decisions that need to be made to improve and grow that company.

There are a lot of duties that the management accountant will do. They will help with planning and budgeting, risk management, external financial reporting, profitability analysis, and so much more. These professionals not only need some technical accounting skills, but they need to have some ability to organize the information and then present it so that the business executives can easily read through it.

Cost Accountant

Businesses are always on the lookout to improve as many processes as possible in order to save more money. This is where a cost accountant can come in and help. These professionals are responsible for looking through each expense that is associated with the supply chain of the company and then do a profitability analysis. They will then finish this information with preparation for a budget.

The cost accountant is going to analyze every cost that is related to administration, production, shipping, materials, and labor. This information will then be put together and given to the leaders of the business, showing them the best ways to improve how they are doing financially.

Government Accountant

All forms of government need accountants to help them keep track of money. Whether we are looking at district governments, city, county, state, or the federal government, they all need to have an accountant to keep track of the money they take in and that goes out.

The government accountant has a duty to make sure that the money that comes in from the taxpayers is spent in the wisest and most prudent manner. They may be able to help the elected officials do the activities that they promised on the campaign trail and can give advice on the right way to proceed financially without wasting a lot of money in the process. They can also help the agency they work for plan out their financial activities for the year. Some of these accountants are going to work for the Internal Revenue Service and will be in charge of auditing private businesses and individuals.

As a government accountant, you will need to have a bachelor's degree in accounting. It is common for these professionals to also have a master's degree. The type of degree can vary but will include finance, taxation, or accounting.

Project Accountant

A project accountant is the one who is going to be more of a freelancer and will work with the company on a project by project basis. They are going to oversee the costs of a project, including approving all the expenses, preparing and then collecting on the invoice, verifying all the billable hours, planning and sticking to the budget, and making sure that the team is able to meet all the deadlines on the project.

These types of accountants are going to have a minimum of a bachelor's degree in accounting. Depending on the employer, you may also need to get some other kind of certification, such as your CMA or CPA credentials.

Investment Accountant

Investment accountants get to spend their time working in the fields of investment and finance. Investment accountants are going to work for either an asset management firm or a brokerage firm. These accountants need to have a lot of information about currencies, ETFs, bonds, stocks, and other forms of investments.

The primary work of an investment accountant is to take care of all the investments for a client while still making sure these investments follow all state regulations. They are also going to be responsible for helping to develop the financial strategy for the company.

If you wish to be an investment accountant, you need to have a degree in something like economics or accounting. Many of these types of investors are going to also earn their CPA credentials, and they can choose to also become a personal financial specialist.

Staff Accountant

Staff Accountant is one of the most common types of accountants. These are going to be the generalists of accounting. They can help a company out with many different responsibilities, including preparing all the financial statements, maintaining the general and the subsidiary accounts for a company, doing all the account reconciliation, cash management, maintaining payroll records and more.

Staff accountants that are going to work at small businesses often do more bookkeeping duties instead of accounting duties. Those that work in one of the larger companies with this title are going to perform some supervisory duties. When you are a staff accountant, you will have a lot of different job duties depending on the company and what they require from their accountant at the time. You will typically need to get a bachelor's degree in accounting in order to get this kind of position.

Chapter 4:

The Income Statement

As we mentioned a little bit before, accounting is going to be in charge of creating a few important financial reports. They are able to use the information they are provided by the bookkeeper and then will put that information into these statements so it is easier to understand and read through.

These financial statements are very important to a business. First off, they are required by the SEC for any company that is publicly traded so having an accountant go through your records and create them can be important. These documents are often seen by potential investors and lenders. Having these documents available can ensure that the investors will choose to purchase your stocks, or that the lenders are willing to loan you money if it is needed at some point.

These three financial statements are all important, but they will show off different financial information about the company. The three financial statements that we are going to take a look at over the next few chapters of this guidebook includes all of the financial documents that the business needs to maintain their transparency.

First, we will get started with the income statement. This is the statement that is going to be the part of the financial statement that is required to report a company's financial performance over a certain amount of time. Sometimes, this is each month or some other time frame, but most of the time, it will be over a quarter and then done when the business reaches its fiscal year.

The financial performance of a company is going to be analyzed by providing a good summary of how the business will incur both its expenses and its revenues. This information comes from both the non-operating and operating activities. This document is also important because it will show the net profit or the net loss that the business incurred over a specific accounting period.

How to Break Down the Income Statement

This document can go by other names, including the statement of revenue and expense, or as the profit and loss statement. It is also one of the major financial statements that a business is going to present in their 10-K and their annual report. All of the public companies need to submit these legal documents to the SEC or the Securities and Exchange Commission. These also need to be released out to the investor public.

Along with the other two documents, we will discuss here, the income statement will provide any lenders and investors with all the information they need about how the company is doing financially. However, the income statement is unique because it will be the only one out of the three that can also provide a summary of the net income and the company sales at that specific time.

Income Statement

While the income statement is presented along with using the balance sheet, it will be able to cover time a little bit differently. The first sheet will just cover one moment out of time. The moment that the accountant is preparing the balance sheet is the moment that will show up on that statement. However, the income statement is a bit different because it will show you information over a period of time and not just how it is doing at one specific time. This time period is usually over a month, a quarter, or even up to a year. It will begin with the sales of the business and then keeps working down until it reaches the net earnings and the net income of each share for that company.

When you work on the income statement, there are two parts that need to be present; the non-operating and the operating. First, we need to look at the operating costs that are found on the income statement. These operating costs are going to list out and disclose the information that concerns the expenses and the revenues that come right from regular business operations. If you run a fast food restaurant, the operating costs could include the amount that you made selling the food and drink items at the establishment. You can list out all the income and the earnings that you made that directly relate to your business in this part.

You also need to include any non-operating income on the income statement. This section is going to show the revenue and the expenses that the business does, but which don't directly come with the regular operations of the business. So, if the fast food restaurant rents out parking spots for the apartments next door to use, and they make money from that, then this information would go in the non-operating section of your income statement.

Uses for the Income Statement

There are many different uses for the income statement. First, many analysts will use this statement in order to get the data they need to calculate financial ratios. They can use this to get earnings before interest taxes and amortization, earnings before you pay taxes and interest, any operating profit, the gross profit, the return on an asset, and the return on equity. As you can see, there are a lot of different numbers that can come on the income statement, and analysts will use these to figure out the financial health of the company.

Companies can also use the income statement. It is common for them to present the income statement in a common-sized format, where each line item will be shown as a percent of the sales. When it is done in this format, it makes things easier on an analyst to see which of the expenses of a company make up the biggest portion of the sales. In addition, analysts can use this income statement to help compare how the company is doing from one year to another or from one quarter to another. One thing you will notice about the income statement is that it will typically have two or three years of data about the company, so it is easier for comparisons when needed.

Many investors will choose to work with the income statement to help them determine whether one company or another is the right one for them to invest in. They can take a look at how much money the business makes, how much debt the company has, and whether these numbers are reasonable or if they show signs that the business is having trouble. Presenting a good income statement can make a difference in how many investors you attract into the company and how valuable your stocks are.

Your lenders, or potential lenders, will also take a look at the income statement. Even if you are making good profits, there may be times when you need to get a loan. You may need to do an expansion, hire some extra employees for a busy season, or do something else that will require a loan. Having a good income statement can make it easier to get the loan that you need when you need it the most.

The Methods for Creating Your Income Statement

There are two main formats that you can choose for your income statement to help present your financial information. These include the single-step and the multi-step format. In the multi-step format, there will be four different measures that can look at profitability, and these will be shown at the right junctions for the operations of the company. These junctions will include after tax, pretax, operating, and gross.

When you work with the single-step option, your gross income, as well as the operating income, will not be shown. You can choose to use the information that is shown to calculate these numbers. This method will have you take the sales and then minus the materials and production to be what equals the gross income of the company. You can then subtract the marketing and administrative, and also the R&D expenses if you have them, from your gross income to come up with the operating income for the business.

This is pretty easy to figure out, so it's not a big deal to use this one if you wish. If you are an investor looking through the income statement, you need to realize that this statement is going to look at any revenues for the business at the time they are realized. This means they look at when the goods are on their way to the customer, whenever a service is rendered, or when the business incurs the expenses.

Let's take a look at some of the categories that will be found in each of these methods to help you see how they are similar and how they are different from each other:

Multi-Step Format	Single-Step Format
Net sales	Net sales
Cost of sales	Materials and production
Gross income	Marketing and administrative
Selling, general and administrative expenses (SG&A)	Research and development expenses
Operating income	Other income and expenses
Other income and expenses	Pretax income
Pretax income	Taxes
Taxes	Net income
Net income (after tax)	

You can use either of these two methods to help you create your own income statement as long as you stick with one and don't get the parts mixed up. You may also need to change a few things around on some of the other financial documents to get the answers that you want, but both of these will work for a business. If you are uncertain about which method to go with, you may want to talk to a professional accountant and see what they recommend for your business or your industry.

The Accounts Found on the Income Statement

Most accountants are going to work on the multi-format method when it comes to writing out the income statement. This can make it easier for the numbers to show up and can ensure that investors are going to be able to see the information right out front rather than having to go through and figure out the numbers on their own. Some of the parts that come with the multi-step format on the income statement include:

- Net sales: This can also be known as sales or revenue. This is the term that refers to the value of the sales of a company or its services to the customer. Even though the bottom line of the company or the net income often ends up getting more investors to look at it, the very top is where you will see the income part start. Also, profit margins on the existing products of that company will eventually reach a maximum that will be hard for the company to improve on. This basically means that the company will not be able to grow faster than any revenue from the business.

- Cost of sales: This is how much it costs the business for any goods or products sold. For a manufacturing company, the cost of sales will be an expense that had to be taken on to deal with everything that helps the product be produced. The depreciation expense is going to be in this part as well. With retailers and wholesalers, you will see that this is the purchase of merchandise that is sold in the store. In a business that is service businesses, the cost would be how much it cost the business to offer their services to the customer.

- Gross profit: This can also be known as gross margin or gross income. The gross profit of a company is going to not only show the difference that shows up between your net sales and what the sales cost the company. The gross profits can provide you with all the resources to cover all the expenses for the company. The greater and the more stable this gross margin is, the greater potential there is for a good bottom line for the company.

- Selling, general, and administrative expenses: This one is going to be referred to as the SG&A in the accounting world. This account is going to hold onto all the operating expenses for the company.

- Operating income: When you deduct SG&A from the gross profit of the company, you will get the operating income. This is an important figure because it can show the earnings from the company's normal operations before the non-operating income and the costs like special items, taxes, and interest expenses. Income at this level, which is often seen as a more reliable number, is going to be used more often by financial analysts instead of using the net income to help measure how profitable a business is.

- Interest expense: This is the item that will show the cost of the company borrowing money. Sometimes, a company can choose to record their net figure here to hold onto interest expense and the interest income when they have invested funds.

- Pretax income: Another indicator that can show how well a business is doing is to look at the earnings that are garnered before the income tax expense. Numerous techniques are there to help a company to minimize or avoid the taxes that they report on their income. Since these are actions that don't help the operations of that particular business, the analysts may want to choose to go with pretax income because it can be more accurate at measuring the profitability of that company.

- Income taxes: The income tax is often not going to be the amount that the company actually pays. Since there are deductions and other things for the company to do to reduce their taxes, this number is just an estimate. It often goes into an account that is created to help the company cover their taxes, but they can often get it lower.

- Special items: There are some events that can occasionally be charged against the income of the company. The company can identify these as discontinued operations, unusual items, or restructuring charges. These are write-offs that should just be one-time events. Any investor that looks at your company should look at these items and consider them when looking at a company because sometimes, they can distort the evaluation.

- Net income: This is also known as the net earnings or the net profit. This is going to be the bottom line for the company, and it is going to be the most common indicator of how profitable the company is. If the expenses exceed the income, then you will have a net loss. After that, the company pays out the dividends that are preferred stockholders if there are any, and then the net income is going to add to the equity position of the company and turns into retained earnings. There is sometimes some supplemental data presented for net income on the basis of potential conversion of stocks, basis of shares outstanding, and warrants.

- Comprehensive income: This concept is going to consider the effects of some things including unrealized gains and losses, the minimum pension liability, foreign currency adjustments, and more. The investment community is mostly going to keep focusing on the net income figure that we talked about before. The adjustment items that come with comprehensive income will all relate to a market that is volatile or an economic event that is out of control of the management at the time. The impact at that specific time can be huge, but over time, they are going to even out and won't matter that much.

Chapter 5:

The Balance Sheet

A balance sheet is going to show the assets of the company, the liabilities of the company, and the net worth, or the owner's equity. The balance sheet will work along with the other financial documents that we have talked about in order to show a complete picture of the financial state of that company. If you hold onto stocks of that company, it is a good idea to understand more about the balance sheet, such as how it is structured, the best ways to look over and understand the sheet, and even tips for reading through the balance sheet.

How Can I Use this Financial Document?

The balance sheet is going to be split up into two parts. These two parts are going to be based on an equation, and they must either end up equaling each other or coming out so that they are balanced, or something is wrong with your numbers. The formula that is needed to work with the balance sheet will include:

$$Assets = Liabilities + Shareholder's\ Equity$$

What all this means is that all the assets, or the money used to operate the company, need to be balanced out by the financial obligations of the company, along with any of the equity investment that comes back to that company, and then they will be known as that company's retained earnings.

The assets are important because they are what the company will use in order to operate the business. The equity and the liabilities are going to be what will support those assets. The owner's equity, which can be known as the shareholder's equity, if the company is publicly traded, will include any of the money that the shareholders invested in that company. It can also include any retained earnings as well. This is important because it is going to represent the funding sources for that particular business.

One way that the balance sheet is different than the income statement we talked about before is that the balance sheet we talked about earlier is more of a snapshot that showcases the financial position of that company right then and there. If the accountant does this financial document on May 21, 2018, then the balance sheet will show where the company is on that date. It won't cover February 21 to May 21. It just shows May 21.

The Balance Sheet for the Securities and Exchange Commission

Just like the bank wants you to put together a balance sheet to take a look at whether they think you can do well with any credit they offer, the government is going to require that any company that is traded publicly will put together a balance sheet, usually each quarter, to show to their shareholders.

This balance sheet can be important because it will allow all potential and current investors to see a good snapshot of the finances of that company. In addition to some other things, the balance sheet is going to show you all the value of the stuff that the company owns, right down to the office supplies that the employees use, the amount of debt that the company is taking care of right now, and how much inventory is in the warehouse. It can even tell the investors about how much money the business will have available to work with through the short-term.

This balance statement is going to be one of the first financial statements that you should analyze when you want to see the value of the company. Before you can learn how to analyze this balance sheet, it is important to know how it is structured.

Before we get into this too much though, you need to understand that the limited partnership, limited liability company, and the corporation balance sheets are going to be a lot different from the regular household balance sheet. This is mainly because these companies have a lot of complex items in their accounting records to keep the company going. This is why many of these companies rely on an accountant to help them get it done.

Businesses are often faced with many difficult questions that others may not know the answers to, such as how to depreciate out the costs for some of their business expenses, how to record the lease obligations, how to account for the expenses of construction at the power plan, and so much more.

No matter how overwhelming it can seem in the beginning to figure out all the different parts of the balance sheet, it is actually pretty simple once you have looked at a few. The best way to get through the balance sheet is to remember that the purpose of this financial statement is to answer three basic questions for anyone who is looking at that sheet. These three main questions that the balance sheet should answer include:

What does the company have? These will be the assets of the company.

What does the company owe on? These will be the liabilities of the company.

What is left over for the owners of that business if they were to pay off all their debts? This one is going to be the shareholder equity or the book value.

These are pretty advanced terms and fancy words, but they are there to help give the investor a good idea of where the business is at that time. If you can remember the objective of the balance sheet, all those fancy words and accounting complexities won't seem as overwhelming when you take a look over it later.

One thing to remember is that unlike some of the other financial statements, the balance sheet is not going to cover a range of dates. The information that is present in the balance sheet is going to be good as of the date that is on the balance sheet, but it won't be able to tell you any date ranges in the process. If you are looking to deal with this issue when calculating many of the accounting ratios, then the best way to do this is to work with the averagely weighted figures of the balance sheet.

An example of this is if you would like to figure out what the average value of inventory was for that year for the company. You would be able to do this by taking the value of the inventory at the previous yearend, add it to the inventory's value at the end of this year, and then divide them by two.

This is a quick trick that will help you to avoid any distortions by ending period figures that may or may not be able to accurately reflect what occurred throughout that year. For example, if the manufacturing business was able to pay off all the debt it had in the year and this showed that there was $0 in liabilities on this balance sheet, but then there was a line there to show the interest expense on your income statement, this could be confusing.

By taking the time to weigh the average debt outstanding from the balance sheet over that same period, you may be able to get a better idea of what the business has going on here and why they listed some interest costs on the income statement but not on the balance sheet.

What Are the Different Types of Assets?

Next, we need to take a look at some of the assets that the company needs to keep track of. Remember that these assets are going to help the company do its normal operations. There are two types of assets that each business will need to pay attention to including current assets and non-current assets.

Current Assets

Current assets are going to be any that the company owns that have a lifespan that is a year or less. This means that the asset has to be easily changed over to cash if the company needs to.

Such assets will include inventory, accounts receivable, and cash or cash equivalents.

Cash, which is the most fundamental and most commonly thought about the current asset, can also include checks and bank accounts that are not restricted. Cash equivalents are going to be assets that are very safe, but which can also be turned into cash quickly if the company needs. The U.S. Treasury is a good example of this. And then there are the accounts receivables, which are going to show the reader any of the obligations that customers and others owe to the company over the short-term. These sometimes happen if a company allows the customer to use credit to purchase the product or service.

Inventory is an important current asset as well. Inventory can include things like the raw materials to make a product, the products that are still in the process of being created, and the finished goods. Each company is going to be different, and the exact way that the inventory account looks is going to be different. For a manufacturing firm, there may be a lot of raw materials, but a retained firm wouldn't have any raw materials.

Non-Current Assets

These non-current assets are going to be any that you are not able to turn into cash very easily, which the company doesn't plan to turn into cash soon. These also include items that will last more than a year. Tangible assets such as land and buildings are included in this. Sometimes, the intangible items will be added to this as well.

What Are the Different Liabilities?

Another part of the balance sheet is the liabilities. These are going to be any financial obligations that the company owes to an outside party. Similar to the assets above, these will fall under the idea of being either a current liability or one that will last long-term.

The long-term liabilities are going to be any of the debts that the company has that will be due in more than a year from that balance sheet date. The current liabilities though are going to be any liabilities that need to be paid off within a year. This could include some of the shorter-term borrowings or even the latest interest that you paid on a longer loan.

The company needs to properly list out all the liabilities that they have on this balance sheet. This helps the investor or the lender know how many debts and obligations that the company is dealing with, and then they can compare this to the profits of the company to see where the company stands financially. This information is much more important to making sound decisions for the investor or the lender compared to just looking at the profits.

For example, a company may have some great profits, but if they have such high debts that they can barely keep up with them, then those high profits don't mean anything. The investors and lenders want to make sure that the company is able to handle their debts and pay them off, while still making a profit and paying their investors before they put any money into it.

Shareholders' Equity

The shareholder's equity is going to be the beginning amount of money that the owners and others put into the business. If at the end of that year, the company wants to take their net earnings and reinvest it back into the company, then these earnings need to move over to your income statement and then placed into the equity account for the shareholder to make it work. This account is important because it will represent the net worth of the company.

The balance sheet is so important to a business. It gives a great snapshot of the finances of a business and can give analysts, investors, and lenders a good idea of where the business stands financially. Filling it out properly is going to make a big difference in how people view your company.

Chapter 6:

The Cash Flow Statement

The third document that needs to be found in the financial report of a business is the cash flow statement. This is going to be an important financial statement because it will showcase the amount of cash and cash equivalents that will enter or leave that company. This statement can also measure how well the company can manage its cash position. This means that it shows the capability of the company to earn money or cash and then put that money toward all the debts and other obligations that are needed to fund any expenses to keep the business going.

This statement will help finish out the financial statements of the company, along with the income statement and the balance sheet, and it is mandatory that all three of these documents are presented.

What ways can I use this statement?

There are a variety of reasons that this statement can help out a business. First, the cash flow statement is there to help any investor to understand how well the company is running its operations. It can also explain where the company is getting its money from and how they are spending that money. The cash flow statement is so important because it can be used to help investors determine how financially secure the company is at that time and whether it is a smart decision to invest with them.

Investors are not the only ones who can rely on the cash flow statement. Many creditors will use the cash flow statement to help determine how much cash is available. This is referred to as the liquidity of the company. This cash needs to be used to help the company fund any operating expenses that it has and pay off its debts.

The Structure of Your Cash Flow Statement

When an accountant designs a cash flow statement for any business, there are some components or categories that need to be present in this document for it to be complete. These four components include:

- Any cash the company gets from operating activities.
- Any cash that the company gets from its investing activities.
- Any cash that the company gets from financing activities.
- This category includes any activities that are non-cash. These are sometimes included, and it will depend on the rules found under GAAP, or the generally accepted accounting principles.

One thing to note here is that the cash flow statement is going to be different from the other financial documents that we talked about before. The main reason for this is because the cash flow statement is not going to have information about all cash that may happen in the future that is recorded as a credit. Because of this, cash is not going to be considered the same thing as net income.

Operating Activities

Now we need to break down the components of the cash flow statement so we know what needs to go into each part. The operating activities will be first. These operating activities found on the cash flow statement will be any sources as well as uses of cash from the business activities of that company. To make it easy, this is going to reflect how much cash that company is able to generate through doing business or offering their products and services to the customer.

Generally, any of the changes that the company makes in cash, depreciation, accounts payable, inventory, and accounts receivable can be reflected in cash from operations. Some examples of the operating activities of the company would include:

- Any payments for rent
- The payments you make for wages and salary to the employees.
- Payments that you make for suppliers for the services and goods that you use in production.
- Any tax payments you make on income.
- Any interest payments you make on loans or your mortgage.
- Receipts from any sales of the services or goods you sell.

When it comes to the trading portfolio, or if it is an investment company, it would have receipts about debt or equity instruments and receipts from the sale of a loan can be included. When you try to prepare this cash flow statement under the indirect method (we will talk about this method in a bit), things like deferred tax, any losses or gains that the company may get from assets that are noncurrent, amortization, depreciation, and dividends that come from the investment opportunities of the company and more can be included. However, with this indirect method, purchase or any sales of your long-term assets can't be counted under the operating activities.

How Can I Calculate My Cash Flow?

Now we need to learn how to calculate the cash flow of a company. The cash flow is going to be calculated simply by making certain adjustments to the net income for that company. You can do this by either subtracting or adding the differences in credit transactions, expenses, and revenue that come from any transaction that will occur between two accounting time periods. The numbers that you will use are found on several of the financial documents to help you get started.

These adjustments need to be made because there are some non-cash items that have been calculated into the net income (found on the income statement) as well as into the liabilities and the total assets (which is found on the balance sheet). So, since not all of your transactions are going to involve some actual cash items, then you need to re-evaluate some of the items to come up with an accurate number for cash flow from operations.

Because you have to go through and make some changes to get an accurate number, there are going to be two main methods that accountants can use to make sure that you are able to come up with the cash flow numbers. The two main methods are the direct and then the indirect method.

With the direct method, you are going to get all of your cash payments and receipts and add them up. This information can include cash that you paid to suppliers, cash that you paid to your employees for salaries and cash receipts from the customer. These figures are going to be calculated by using the end and the beginning balances from your different business accounts, and then you can check whether there is an increase or a decrease in the net amounts of these accounts.

You can also choose to work with the indirect method. In this method, the cash flow from all of your operating activities will be calculated. You will first take the net income off the income statement. Because this income statement for the company will be prepared on what is known as an accrual basis. When you use this method, the revenue for that company is only recognized at the time it is earned rather than at the time it is received.

Because of this information, the net income is not always the best representation of how the company's cash flow is doing. This is why you will need to go through and make some adjustments for any of the items that will affect your net income. Yes, the company is still waiting to receive cash for the product or service, but it still needs adjustment.

With the indirect method, you will also need to make adjustments to make sure that some of your non-operating activities are added back in. An example of doing this would be with depreciation. Since this depreciation of assets is not seen in most cases as a cash expense, it needs to be added back in with the total you receive on the net sales during that cash flow calculation. You only want to add this asset into your statement when it is time to sell it.

The amount that the accounts receivable decreases is then going to be added into the net sales is how many customers paid off their credit accounts that time period, and that number needs to be added to the net sales of the company.

But if there is an increase between one period of accounting to another in the accounts receivable, then the amount needs to be deducted from your net sales. Even though the amounts are counted as revenue in the accounts receivable, they are not really cash, so it shouldn't show up on the cash flow statement.

The change in inventory is also another thing to go through and check on. When the company has an increase in the amount of inventory they have, it could signal that the company spent more of their money to purchase the raw materials that they need to make the products. If the inventory was paid off with cash, then the increase in this inventory needs to be taken from your net sales. A decrease in the amount of inventory that you have is added over to the net sales part of the statement. If you ended up purchasing some inventory and did so on credit, then you need to see an increase in the accounts payable section. Then you need to have the increased amount from the past year put in with the net sales.

This same process is going to work with other parts of your company as well. It could work for prepaid insurance, salaries payable, taxes payable, and more. If you pay something off, then you will subtract the difference in value that you owed from one year to the following one from the net income. But if you still have some that is owed on that item, then this difference needs to be added to the net earnings.

The Investing Activities and Your Cash Flow Statement

Some of the investing activities that the company partakes in can be used on the cash flow statement as well. Investing activities can be any source or any use of the cash from any investments the company participates in. These may include things like purchasing a new asset, loans that are made to a vendor, a loan that is received from customers, or any payments that the company receives because of an acquisition or a merger. In short, any changes that occur from investments, assets, or equipment will relate to the cash you have from investing.

In most cases, any changes in cash because of your investments are just going to end with a cash out of the item, mostly because you took that cash and used it to purchase buildings, new equipment, or even some shorter term assets, like a marketable security. However, if your company decides to divest an asset, then this transaction is going to be called cash in for helping you calculate your cash from investing.

Financing Activities and Your Cash Flow Statement

Cash that comes from the financing activities on your cash flow statement will include the sources of cash from investors or bank, and it can also include uses of cash that you paid out to the shareholders. Payments for repurchasing stocks, payment for dividends, and repayment of debts or loans can all be added to this category.

If you have some changes in cash from this financing, then you are cashing in whenever the capital rises, but then cashed out when the dividends are paid. So, if a company issues out a bond to the public, then the company will receive some cash for that financing. However, when they have to pay out some interest to the bondholders, the company will reduce the amount of cash that it has control over at that time.

Tying Together the Income Statement, the Balance Sheet, and the Cash Flow Statement

As we mentioned earlier in this chapter, the cash flow statement is going to rely on the balance sheet and the income statement to come up with the numbers that you will use in your calculations. You may need to make some changes to the numbers to get an accurate value, but if you filled out your balance sheet and your income statement properly, then you will have the information that you need to start on the cash flow statement.

Net earnings that are found in the income statement will be used as the figure for the cash flow statement. Without this information, or with the wrong information, then the information is going to show up wrong on the cash flow statement as well.

In regard to this balance sheet, your net cash flow is going be measurable as well. If the cash decreased or increased between your balance sheets, then the net cash flow needs to change the same amount, or something is wrong. So, if you are trying to come up with the cash flow for 2017, then you would use all the balance sheets from 2016 to 2017 to help you get the right information.

The cash flow statement is an important document, which is why it is included along with the other financial documents for a company. This statement is going to measure the strength, the profitability, and the outlook over the long-term for the company. The cash flow statement can help an investor, a manager, and others determine whether the company has enough cash and that the cash is liquid enough to pay off its expenses. A company can often rely on this cash flow statement to predict how their cash flow might be at a future time, which can be so important when they are working on things like budgeting for the future of that company.

For investors, the cash flow statement is a major tool that investors and managers like to work with. Since the cash flow statement is going to reflect the financial health of the company, since it is typical that when a company has more cash, then the better off they are doing. However, there are some times when this rule doesn't really work for the business. For example, there are times when a company will have a negative cash flow because of the growth strategy they chose. If the company expands its operations, it may eliminate some of its cash flow, but it will quickly gain those back and more once the operations are up and running.

When an investor takes the time to study the cash flow statement, the investor is going to get one of the best pictures of how much cash the company is able to generate. They get a good understanding of how financially secure the company is at that time. And it can help them to choose whether or not they want to invest in that company.

Chapter 7:

Tax Accounting

No matter what kind of business you run, there will come a time when you need to file your taxes. In your first year, you may not need to do this as you get things organized and up and running. But after that, or once you owe $1000 or more to the IRS if you are a sole proprietorship, then you will need to pay your taxes each quarter.

Having accurate records and filling out the income statement, the balance sheet, and the cash flow statement can make it easier to do your taxes. You can just insert the numbers into your tax forms, and you can use this information to help you get the deductions to save you even more.

With the help of your accountant, you will be able to take all of the documents that you have and get your tax documents all set up and ready. Let's take a look at tax accounting, how it works, and why it is so important to your business to get this done.

What Is Tax Accounting?

Tax accounting is a subset of accounting. It is going to focus on preparing and handling taxes rather than the public financial statements of the company. Tax accounting is going to be governed by the Internal Revenue Code, which will dictate the specific rules that all individuals and companies need to follow when they work on their tax returns.

Tax accounting is a basic means of accounting to help get taxes done. It can actually apply to everyone, including corporations, business, individuals, and other entities. Even those who have exemptions for paying taxes need to do some tax accounting. The purpose of this kind of accounting is to be able to track the funds of the company, including those that go out and those that come in, associated with entities and with individuals.

Having proof of all this information can be really helpful at tax time. Even if your income was small enough, or you had enough deductions or both to not pay taxes, it is going to be helpful to have a record of all the funds coming in and out of your business. You can keep track of how your business is doing and can prove your income if you are ever audited in the future.

The Tax Principles vs. GAAP

If you own a business or do accounting in the United States, you will notice that there are going to be two main sets of principles that can be used. These two rules are different, and you should not confuse them. The first is going to be principles that are used specifically in tax accounting, and the second ones will be for a financial account in general.

Under the rules of GAAP, all companies will need to follow a common set of procedures, standards, and principles in their accounting any time that they compile a financial statement and with all of their financial transactions. The GAAP rules will list out all the rules that you need to follow in order to write your balance sheets, income statement, and cash flow statement. There are various different rules that you will need to follow with GAAP, and it ensures that companies are going to record their financial information and that there is some unity between the financial statements.

While accounting is going to have a little bit to do with all of the financial transactions, tax accounting is going to focus all its energy on transactions that will affect the tax burden of a company, and how those items will relate to proper tax calculations and preparation with tax documents.

Tax accounting has some regulations placed on it and is regulated by the IRS to make sure that all of the tax laws are followed by individual taxpayers and tax accounting professionals. The IRS is also going to use specific documents and forms so that you can submit the tax information properly as the law requires from you.

Tax Accounting and How It Works for an Individual

Tax accounting can work for both individuals and for businesses. First, we are going to look at tax accounting and how it works for an individual. As an individual who pays taxes, tax accounting is going to focus mostly on items like the income of the individual, the deductions that they qualify for, any investments that they earned or lost on, and some other transactions that will affect how much you pay taxes.

This is a good thing because it is going to help limit the amount of information that individuals need to manage to finish their tax return. You don't have to go through and keep receipts of every transaction that you make for example. If you make a big purchase, you keep that receipt, but a grocery store trip isn't one that you need to keep track of at all. This makes it easier for most individuals to get their tax returns done without all the work.

With general accounting, the individual would have to go through a lot more work. General accounting would mean that you need to track all the funds that come in and then go out of the person's possession, no matter what the purpose. If you got some clothes, you would have to write that on the tax return. If you went out to eat, you would have to write that out as well. You would have to write out everything that is a personal expense even if those expenses had no tax implications.

With tax accounting, you only have to keep track of a few things for the year. You keep track of any income that you make either from investments, from a job or other sources. And then you keep track of the items that can be deducted from your taxes to reduce your tax burden. And then that is it.

Tax Accounting for a Business

Businesses are often going to benefit the most from tax accounting. Tax accounting is going to help a business to keep track of everything that it needs to use for tax purposes. It can also help them to get as many tax deductions as possible in order to save them money.

From the perspective of a business, more information needs to be analyzed to finish the process for tax accounting. While the company needs to track its incoming funds and earnings, similar to what the individual has to do, there is also another level of complexity that comes with business tax accounting. This comes with outgoing funds that are directed toward the obligations of the business.

There are a lot of different parts that the business needs to keep track of for tax accounting. This sometimes includes funds that are directed toward specific expenses of the business, or the funds that are directed out to the shareholders of the business.

While a business doesn't have to use a tax accountant to do these duties, many larger organizations will have one. Tax accounting is going to be pretty complex. The larger your business is, the more complex the tax accounting process will be and having a tax accountant can help make this easier.

How Tax Accounting Works for Organizations Exempt from Taxes

There are some entities or businesses that are going to be exempt from taxes. Even in these instances, the business will need to perform tax accounting. This is mainly due to the fact that all businesses need to file an annual term. This is true no matter how much they owe in taxes and even if they are tax-exempt for the year.

These businesses will need to provide information that is in regard to their incoming funds, such as any donations or grants that the business gets. They will then need to explain how they will use these funds to help them operate during the year.

The point of doing this is to ensure that these businesses are following all the regulations and laws that govern the way that a tax-exempt business can run and operate. Even though these businesses will not end up having to pay any taxes, regardless of how much they make during the year, it is important to fill out the return and keep track of the information. This can show the IRS that you are using all your funds properly.

Tax accounting can be a difficult part to work on. There are a lot of rules and regulations that a business must adhere to and making sure that everything is filed right with the IRS is important. Hiring a tax accountant can make it easier to get this done without running into trouble at the end of the year.

Chapter 8:

Accounting Software to Consider

There are different types of accounting software that you can choose to work within your business. This accounting software is good for helping a business keep track of their expenses and their income so that they are better prepared to stay on top of the operations and file tax returns that are accurate. Here we are going to explore some of the best options that you can choose when picking out accounting software for your business.

QuickBooks Online

QuickBooks is a name that a lot of people know about, and it can work well for businesses, no matter their shape or size. This tool is especially useful for those who are growing quickly and are looking to expand and need to keep track of a lot of different things. QuickBooks can be used for any type of business, from a sole proprietorship to an LLC, S corporation or a C corporation.

In addition to some of the basic capabilities that your business needs, like running financial statements, paying bills, and invoicing your customers, QuickBooks online has some advanced features that your business may find helpful. It can help you to track your inventory and even create a budget. You can turn on the payroll feature for new employees by going to the Employees tab and then clicking Add Payroll button, and it is ready to go for you.

If you decide that you want to accept credit card payments from customers, you can use the Intuit Merchant Services to create an account, simply by clicking on the Add Payments button. These services do cost a bit more than the standard QuickBooks price, but you can easily add them without any upgrades to the system, and it can really help you to reach more customers.

QuickBooks comes in at a variety of prices depending on which features you want to use and the size of your business. You can start out with QuickBooks Self-Employed and spend $10 a month or go to QuickBooks Plus and spend $60 a month.

There are a lot of great features that come with QuickBooks online, and the Online Plus option has a lot of what you will need. This one comes in at $60 a month, but it is able to help you complete some of the following:

- Prepare some of your key reports such as the cash flow statement, balance sheet, and profit and loss.
- Prepare and issue any 1099s
- Track inventory
- Manage all your accounts payable, or the money owed to your suppliers.
- Manage your accounts receivable, or the amount of money due from customers
- Import bank and credit card transactions
- Track income and expenses.

FreshBooks

Another option that you can go with is known as FreshBooks. This is a good choice for freelancers and solopreneurs, individuals who run their own business but don't have a lot of overhead or employees or other similar things to work with. Individuals who need to invoice their customers or who need an effective method to keep track of the hours they worked on a project for will enjoy using FreshBooks.

FreshBooks has made it easy to create invoices that are customizable, and it even allows the customer to pay for these invoices online. The project tracking system through this software will make it easier than ever to track all the hours that you work, including all the contractors and employees that you may have now or sometime in the future.

The pricing for FreshBooks is a bit different than what we found with QuickBooks. There are just three pricing plans that you can work with ranging from $15 a month to $50 a month. The mid-sized plan, which comes in at $25 a month, is the most popular option and will allow you to bill a maximum of 50 clients each month. Since most freelancers don't have more than this, this makes the perfect option. Some of the other features that are found with the FreshBooks system include:

- Prepare some of the key reports that your business needs, such as profit and loss statements. The cash flow statement and the balance sheet are not available on this platform.
- Schedule recurring invoices
- Project tracking to keep things organized
- Track time and expenses for projects
- Manage your accounts payable
- Manage any of the accounts receivable
- Import all your credit and bank card transactions
- Create your own custom invoices

Out of all the accounting software competitors that are out there, FreshBooks provides you with a lot of flexibility when it comes to creating invoices that work with your brand. With FreshBooks, you have the freedom to adjust your invoice templates, the fonts, and the colors. You are also able to set up payment reminders that go automatically, and it gives you the option to charge any late fees that you want for overdue customer invoices.

Xero

Next on the list is a software that is known as Xero. Xero is an accounting software that will require much of the same functionality that you can get with QuickBooks Online. If you find that QuickBooks is not quite right for you, but you would like to get something similar, then this is a good option. It also works well for those who are running a business that has five or fewer employees to keep track of.

Xero is one of the only programs for accounting that is going to include a full cycle payroll processing, and it can handle this for up to five employees without adding on additional costs to the program. If you need to have all the same tools like QuickBooks, but also have the ability to process your payroll checks, submit your payroll tax payments, or file your payroll tax forms, then this is the software that you need.

The plans that come with Xero are going to range from $9 a month for the starter, $30 a month for the Standard, and $70 a month for the Premium. The Standard is usually fine for most, but if you want to pay more than five employees or you are going to manage multicurrency transactions, then the Premium edition is probably the best choice. Some of the core features that you will like with the Xero system include:

- Prepare all your key reports like profit and loss, the cash flow statement, and the balance sheet.
- Prepare and issue all the 1099s for your employees
- Track the inventory
- Manage your accounts payable
- Manage your accounts receivable
- Import the bank and credit card transactions
- Track income and expenses.

Wave

And next on the list is an accounting software that is known as Wave. Wave is best for any business that is on a tighter budget because it is free. This is often seen as one of the best in free accounting software overall. Wave may be free, but it has quite a few of the features that you want in an accounting software. It does have some limitations, but when it comes to use by single-member businesses and sole proprietors, it is a great option.

There is only one edition of Wave, and this edition is free. You can invite as many users to look at your data as you would like, and you can give them privileges like "edit" or "view only" as you use. But you can't give any other user access to your bank information. Some of the other features that you will enjoy with Wave include:

- Prepare the key reports. The cash flow statement can't be done here, but you can work with the profit and loss statement and the balance sheet.
- A limited ability to pay your bills
- Manage accounts receivable
- Import all your bank and credit card transactions
- Track your income and your expenses.

Chapter 9:

Tips to Use When You Begin with Accounting

Getting a new small business started can be tough. Add in all of the different things that you need to do with accounting, and things can go up and be even more difficult. If you are not used to doing any of these accounting tasks, you may feel like you are treading water and not sure what steps to take next. This chapter is going to explore some of the best accounting tips that you can follow to help your small business thrive.

- KISS: This stands for keep it simple starting out. The simplest form of entity in order to run a business is known as a sole proprietorship. This ownership form is not going to require you to start with special communications or special rules when filing with the

Internal Revenue Service, at least until you start paying some employees. This means that if you are able to, it may be best to stay with that kind of business entity. It can save you time and makes your accounting as simple as possible.

- Make sure to separate out your personal expenses and your business expenses. This is especially important if you are running a sole proprietorship since you are the only individual working in the company. The IRS does not want to know about your personal expense, and you are not allowed to claim these as deductions on your business tax forms. Make sure that they are separated out somehow or use different accounts for each one to help avoid confusion at tax time.

- Track all your business expenses: You never know when a business expense could be used as a tax deduction to help you save money at the end of the year. But you can't claim it as a tax deduction unless you have the proper proof about that expense. Have a good method in place that helps you track all these business expenses so that you can get the deductions that you deserve.

- Have an accurate method for recording deposits to ensure you never lose track. It is your responsibility to have a good method or system in place to deal with the deposits of your company. Leans, cash infusions, and revenue from sales can sometimes get lost when you get busy, and then this will lead to you paying too much in income taxes at the end of the year. With the right accounting practices in place, you can accurately record these without having to worry about whether they will add to your tax burden or not. Consider having a professional accountant to provide you with some of the best practices to record all these deposits.

- Consider hiring a professional to help out. While some small businesses may choose to do the accounting and the bookkeeping on their own, it may be a good idea to invest in one of these professionals to help you out for a few hours during the week. It makes a big difference you will find that your records will quickly be up to date and in order. And a professional is better prepared to handle any potential fees, additional tax deductions, or loopholes that can go in your advantage. Knowing a bit about accounting can help, but sometimes, an accountant is able to do the work a bit better. They can also take all those number and financial information and communicate it in a manner that you will understand better.

- Dedicate some time each week or month to get the books updated. The books are never going to get done if you don't devote some time to working on them. You need to bring out your calendar and then schedule out the time to do this. This makes sure that you get it done before information piles up or gets lost, and then the work becomes a lot harder. Always stick with the time that you set aside so that the books get done.

- Keep tabs on all the costs of labor for the business: One of the largest expenses that your business has to deal with is paying all the employees, and yourself. You will want to keep good tabs on all the money that you spend on labor costs. You should also take good notes of the overtime, the perks, and any other benefits that you offer to your employees. This can help prevent you from overpaying or underpaying in this category.

- Have some money setback for those major expenses: There is always going to be a big expense that pops up and can make it difficult to stay within your budget. Things like tax deadlines, replacing some of your equipment, or doing some major computer upgrades are things that all businesses need to do on occasion, and they should not be surprises to you. In addition, these larger expenses are more likely to show up on those months when business is a little slower. Rather than going into more debt because of these, you should plan ahead for these major expenses in order to avoid issues with a cash crunch.

- Maintain records about your inventory: Keeping track of your inventory is important. It can help you avoid issues like misplacing your merchandise or avoiding theft by having this information present. You will want to note information like dates purchased the stock numbers, the purchase prices, the sales prices, and the dates that the inventory was sold. The more that you can keep this organized in your business, the better.

- Always follow up on your invoices and receivables so you don't have to pay more on taxes with money that you don't make. Just because you sent the customer or the client an invoice doesn't mean that you have received the money yet. You will spend a lot of time going through all your revenue accounts if you don't follow up with these invoices. And it can result in you overpaying on your taxes. You may want to accept things like online payment and cloud-based accounting software. This helps to automate the invoice process for you.

Sometimes, a small business will be able to handle all the accounting on their own. Their records will be small enough that they can deal with it all on their own without the help of someone else. But many times, a professional accountant is needed to make sure that the records are done in the proper manner. Knowing how to handle these tips and the other topics that we have discussed in this guidebook can make this process a lot easier.

Conclusion

Thank you for making it through to the end of *Accounting*. Let's hope it was informative and able to provide you with all of the tools you need to achieve your goals whatever they may be.

The next step is to put some of these practices to work. While you can learn a lot about your business through bookkeeping, it is important to learn some of the different parts of accounting as well. This can help you to create all the financial statements that are required by law, can help you to be prepared during tax time, and so much more. When you are ready to implement your own bookkeeping system and want to make sure that your financial records are all in place, check out this guidebook to help you get started!

Finally, if you found this book useful in any way, a review is always appreciated!